Countries Around the World

Poland

Charlotte Guillain

Raintree

www.raintreepublishers.co.uk
Visit our website to find out
more information about
Raintree books.

To order:

☎ Phone 0845 6044371

📄 Fax +44 (0) 1865 312263

🖥 Email myorders@raintreepublishers.co.uk

Customers from outside the UK please telephone +44 1865 312262

Raintree is an imprint of Capstone Global Library Limited, a
company incorporated in England and Wales having its registered
office at 7 Pilgrim Street, London, EC4V 6LB – Registered company
number: 6695582

Text © Capstone Global Library Limited 2012
First published in hardback in 2012
Paperback edition first published in 2013
The moral rights of the proprietor have been asserted.

Edited by Kate de Villiers and Vaarunika Dharmapala
Designed by Joanna Hinton-Malivoire
Original illustrations © Capstone Global Library Ltd 2011
Illustrated by Oxford Designers & Illustrators
Picture research by Ruth Blair
Originated by Capstone Global Library Ltd
Printed and bound in China by CTPS

ISBN 978 1 406 22797 0 (hardback)
15 14 13 12 11
10 9 8 7 6 5 4 3 2 1

ISBN 978 1 406 22826 7 (paperback)
16 15 14 13 12
10 9 8 7 6 5 4 3 2 1

British Library Cataloguing in Publication Data
Guillain, Charlotte.
Poland. -- (Countries around the world)
943.8'057-dc22
A full catalogue record for this book is available from the British
Library.

943. 8057

Acknowledgements
We would like to thank the following for permission to reproduce
photographs: Alamy p. 7 (© Pegaz), p. 15 (© Arco Images GmbH),
p. 26 (© Jenny Matthews); Bridgeman Art Library p. 29 (© Royal
Castle, Warsaw, Poland/Maciej Bronarski); Corbis p. 9 (Bettmann),
p. 11 (© Bettmann), p. 12 (© CEERWAN AZIZ/Reuters), p. 13
(© Peter Turnley), Getty Images p. 10 (Hugo Jaeger/Timepix/Time
Life Pictures), p. 30 (Nick Laham); Shutterstock p. 5 (© puchan),
p. 17 (© WitR), p. 20 (© Adam Gryko), p. 21 (© Tomasz Sowinski),
p. 23 (© Iliuta Goean), p. 25 (© ajt), p. 27 (© Zurijeta), p. 31
(© IgorXIII), p. 33 (© Taratorki), p. 35 (© Gasper Furman), p. 39
(© puchan), p. 46 (© Fotogroove).

Cover photograph of Polish folk dancers reproduced with
permission of Getty Images (© Ashok Sinha).

We would like to thank Daniel Block for his invaluable help in the
preparation of this book.

Every effort has been made to contact copyright holders of material
reproduced in this book. Any omissions will be rectified in
subsequent printings if notice is given to the publisher.

Disclaimer
All the internet addresses (URLs) given in this book were valid at
the time of going to press. However, due to the dynamic nature of
the internet, some addresses may have changed, or sites may have
changed or ceased to exist since publication. While the author
and publisher regret any inconvenience this may cause readers, no
responsibility for any such changes can be accepted by either the
author or the publisher.

Contents

Some words in the book are in bold, **like this**. You can find out what they mean by looking in the glossary.

Introducing Poland

What do you know about Poland? Do you have a friend whose family came from Poland? Do you know where Poland is or how big it is? Would you like to know more about this country's people, history, and geography?

A land of contrasts

Poland is in central Europe. The country covers 312,685 square kilometres (120,728 square miles), making it nearly two and half times as big as the United Kingdom. Its turbulent history stretches back over centuries. Neighbouring countries have often invaded Polish lands.

Poland has many different regions, each with its own special character and traditions. Polish cities are a mix of old and new buildings, and the damage caused long ago by wars and foreign invasions can still be seen today. Visitors to Poland enjoy its beautiful landscapes, traditional **culture**, friendly people, and hearty food.

People on the move

Throughout history, Polish people have travelled around the world. Some have left hoping to find a better life in other countries. However, today many Poles are returning to Poland to share in its success in the 21st century. Read on to find out what makes Poland and its people so special.

MARIE CURIE (1867–1934)

Marie Curie is one of the world's most famous Poles. She left Poland to study in Paris when she was 24. In 1903, she won the **Nobel Prize** for physics with her husband Pierre Curie. They had discovered the **radioactive** elements polonium and radium. She was the first woman to win a Nobel Prize. She won it again in 1911 for her work in chemistry.

The main square in the city of Kraków is full of beautiful buildings.

History: division and resistance

Over a thousand years ago, many **tribes** lived in central Europe. By the
AD 900s, the Polanie tribe had become dominant in the area that is now
called Poland. Duke Mieszko I converted to the **Christian** religion in AD 966
and became the first leader of a Polish nation. The period that followed saw
Polish lands regularly change hands, as rulers in the region fought for power.

A golden age

The region split up again in the 1100s but was reunited in 1320 when
Wladislaw the Elbow-High became king. His son, Kazimierz the Great, was
a great ruler. He built up the cities, founded universities, introduced a new
currency, and set up a system of government. Kazimierz kept Poland's
borders safe and conquered new land in the east. After his death, Poland
was ruled by Queen Jadwiga whose husband was a Lithuanian duke. This
meant the two countries were **allies** for hundreds of years. Lithuania and
Poland became one state in 1569 following the Union of Lublin.

NICOLAUS COPERNICUS
(1473-1543)

Nicolaus Copernicus was born in the city of Toruń. After studying
and becoming a priest, he travelled for several years. He is known
as the founder of modern **astronomy** and was the first scientist to
argue that Earth revolves around the Sun. His ideas were published
only after his death and they were so **controversial** that the church
tried to ban them.

This statue in Kraków shows Queen Jadwiga and her husband King Jagiełło.

HEDVIGES REGINA POLONIÆ IAGELLO MAGNUS DUX LITHUANIÆ

War and division

During the 1600s, Poland and Lithuania suffered through many conflicts. In 1655, Sweden invaded and over the next five years, known as the "Deluge", the country was almost destroyed. Millions were killed by war, **famine**, and disease. Then, Poland and Lithuania helped to fight Turks who were invading Europe, defeating them at the Battle of Vienna in 1683. The country also faced war with Russia, finally signing a peace treaty in 1686. But Poland had been badly weakened by years of conflict.

During the 1700s, Polish lands were split between Russia, **Prussia**, and Austria. Poland did not exist as a separate country for over a century from 1795. Its language and **culture** were seriously damaged. Many Poles **migrated** abroad in search of a better life. Some travelled to France and the United States.

World War I

World War I broke out in Europe in 1914. Polish soldiers fought in the Russian, Prussian, and Austrian armies – often against each other. After the war, the empires that had split up the Polish lands lost their power and Poland became independent again in 1918. From 1919 to 1920, Poland was at war with Russia, gaining land in western Ukraine and Belarus. The country worked hard to rebuild itself and established new borders in 1923.

How to say...

Poland's history of invasions and conquests has introduced new words into its language. Wars against Mongolian armies brought words such as *dzida* (spear) and *szereg* (line or column). Fighting the Turks brought in words such as *jar* (deep valley), *filiżanka* (cup), and *dywan* (carpet). German-speaking powers brought words such as *ratusz* (town hall) and *rycerz* (knight).

Józef Piłsudski was a general who helped Poland to regain its independence in 1918.

World War II

World War II began when **Nazi** Germany invaded Poland in September 1939. Then, the **Soviet Union** invaded eastern Poland. Under Nazi and Soviet rule, many Poles were sent to labour camps or executed. Millions of Polish **Jews** were sent to **concentration camps**, and six million Polish citizens died.

A Polish government-in-exile operated in London, and Poles fought in an underground Home Army against the occupying forces. In August 1944, the Warsaw Uprising was launched against the Germans. Polish fighters unsuccessfully tried to gain control of the capital city before the Soviet army arrived from the east. The uprising lasted over two months, and the city was destroyed by the fighting.

Post-war problems

After the war, Poland was under Soviet control and its borders changed again. In 1947, Poland became a **communist** country. By 1956, people were protesting against low wages in the Poznań riots. The Polish **economy** continued to struggle and, by the late 1970s, workers were protesting again, particularly in the port city of Gdańsk. In 1980, the workers were allowed to form a **trade union** called Solidarity. However, the government banned it the following year.

The German army parades through Warsaw in 1939, watched by the Nazi leader Adolf Hitler (saluting).

These Warsaw Jews are being rounded up by Nazi soldiers.

Daily life

The Nazis created a **ghetto** in Warsaw in 1940. The area was surrounded by barbed wire and brick walls. Thousands of Polish Jews and Gypsies were crammed inside. They had very little to eat and disease spread quickly. Children risked their lives smuggling in food and medicine. When the Nazis started moving people to death camps, there was an uprising. Jewish fighters resisted the Nazis for four weeks. They were eventually crushed and the ghetto was destroyed.

The end of communism

After more protests and strikes, Solidarity became legal again in 1989. Big changes took place across central and eastern Europe as communist countries allowed people more freedom. Elections were held in Poland, and Solidarity took control of government. In 1990, Lech Wałęsa became the first **democratically** elected president of Poland. Proper free elections followed and Poland became a fully democratic nation.

New nation

Poland joined the North Atlantic Treaty Organization (**NATO**) in 1999 and, in 2003, supported the invasion of Iraq led by the United States. The country became a member of the European Union (**EU**) in May 2004, although not everyone in Poland supported this. Membership of the EU means that Polish people are free to live and work in other EU countries, and many have migrated to countries, such as the United Kingdom.

These Polish soldiers were stationed in Iraq.

Back home, the government has faced problems. In 2007, it collapsed and elections were held. The new government created a much more stable country, and even managed to avoid the worst of the global economic **recession**. The Polish people were devastated when their president Lech Kaczynski was killed in a plane crash in 2010.

LECH WAŁĘSA [1943–]

Lech Wałęsa trained as an electrician at the shipyard in Gdańsk. He was a natural leader and helped organize workers' strikes during the 1970s. The government punished him by making sure he lost his job. He was also arrested many times. In 1980, he helped establish the first trade union in communist Poland. Wałęsa won the Nobel Peace Prize in 1983 and became president of a democratic Poland in 1990.

Lech Wałęsa was president of Poland between 1990 and 1995.

Regions and resources: dunes, plains, and mountains

Poland is quite a large country with a varied landscape. It borders the Baltic Sea in the north, there are forests in the east, and mountains in the south. However, most of Poland is made up of a flat **plain**. The capital city, Warsaw, is in the east.

Poland's borders have changed many times throughout history. Warsaw used to be in the west of the country. However, it became an eastern city after World War II, when parts of eastern Poland joined the **Soviet Union** and parts of Germany joined western Poland.

This map shows land heights above and below sea level for Poland and its neighbours.

Poland has borders with many countries. Germany and the Czech **Republic** lie to the west. Along its southern border is Slovakia, with Ukraine and Belarus to the east. Lithuania and Russia border Poland in the north-east. Poland's climate is made up of cold winters and warm summers, with frequent rain in both seasons.

Landscape and features

The Polish coastline stretches over 440 kilometres (273 miles) and includes the port city of Gdańsk. The River Wisła is the longest river, at 1,047 kilometres (651 miles) long. Lake Śniardwy is the largest lake in Poland with an area of 113.8 square kilometres (43.9 square miles). The highest mountain is Rysy in the Tatra mountain range, which stands at 2,499 metres (8,198 feet). A large amount of Polish land is used for agriculture.

These boats are sailing on Lake Śniardwy, the largest lake in Poland.

The regions of Poland

Poland has six major regions:

Mazovia and Lublin

Mazovia is a plain surrounding Warsaw. To the south-east of this lies the region around the city of Lublin. As well as the sandy plain, there are forests and large farms.

North-central Poland

The north-central area of Poland is home to the city of Gdańsk, as well as forests, lakes, and open plains. Białowieża National Park is also found here.

Małopolska

Małopolska is a region in south-east Poland. Much of the land is used for farming, but the beautiful Tatra Mountains in the south are a popular destination for hikers and skiers. The historic city of Kraków is Małopolska's regional capital.

Silesia

Silesia in the south-west of Poland has mountains and hills, but also large industrial areas. The regional capital is Wrocław.

Wielkopolska

Wielkopolska (meaning "Greater Poland") lies in the west of the country. Its landscape varies from hilly areas with forests and lakes to rolling plains. The main city in this region is Poznań.

Pomerania

The coastal region of Pomerania lies in the north-west. It has popular seaside resorts and national parks that boast incredible sand dunes, forests, and wilderness. The largest city in this region is Szczecin.

The Tatra National Park is especially beautiful in the winter.

Daily life

Poland's cities have developed faster than its **rural** villages. Many country people are cut off from **urban** centres by poor roads and communication networks. Rural people who once depended on farming now struggle to make a living. Many young people move to cities to find work. The government is trying to support rural people with better facilities, internet connections, and loans to start small businesses.

The economy

The Polish **economy** became stronger after the end of **communism** and it is now the sixth largest economy in the **EU**. From 1990 to 2009, the economy grew every year and unemployment fell. The country needs to improve roads and railways and reduce **bureaucracy** to develop further. Financial problems hit the whole world in 2008 and this has affected Poland, too, although not as badly as many other European countries.

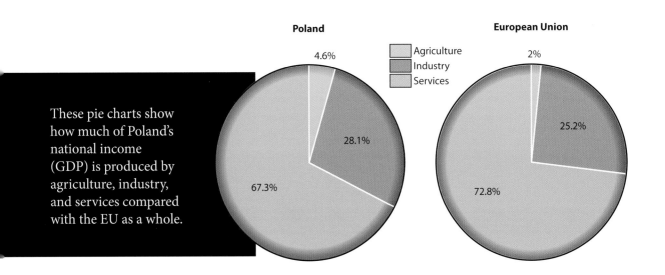

These pie charts show how much of Poland's national income (GDP) is produced by agriculture, industry, and services compared with the EU as a whole.

Industry and natural resources

Polish industries produce and **export** a large range of goods. Factories manufacture machinery, iron and steel, chemicals, glass, and textiles. Many foods are produced and processed in Poland. Coal mining and shipbuilding are also important industries.

Important natural resources found in Poland are coal, sulphur, copper, natural gas, silver, lead, salt, and **amber**. Large areas of Poland are used for agriculture. Polish farmers produce potatoes, fruits, vegetables, and wheat, as well as poultry, eggs, pork, and dairy products.

Key
△ Aluminium
▲ Nickel
△ Zinc
△ Iron and steel
▲ Coal
△ Cement
△ Lead
△ Copper
◯ Natural gas
◯ Salt
◯ Sand
⬤ Crude petroleum
⬤ Petroleum refinery products

This map shows where important minerals can be found in Poland.

YOUNG PEOPLE

After Poland joined the EU in 2004, many young Poles travelled to other European countries to find work. Most of these skilled young people had struggled to find jobs in Poland. They could earn more in other EU countries. As the economy and **infrastructure** in Poland improves, many of these young people are returning home.

Wildlife: bats, bison, and beavers

There are 23 national parks in Poland that together cover around one per cent of the country's total area. These parks are found in mountainous regions, highlands, lowlands, forests, wetlands, and along the coast. In these parks the landscape, animals, and plants are protected, but people can enjoy exploring nature there, too.

The Białowieża Forest National Park in the north-east is home to European bison and includes marshes with many wildfowl. The Słowiński National Park is famous for its sand dunes and wild birds, such as the sea eagle. The Karkonosze Mountains National Park is recognized by **UNESCO** as a World **Biosphere Reserve**.

Herds of European bison thrive in Polish national parks.

The large nests made by white storks can be seen across the Polish landscape.

Polish wildlife

In the west of Poland there is a bat reserve where some very rare bat species can be found. These include the greater mouse-eared, Barbastelle, Bechstein's, whiskered, Natterer's, brown long-eared, and Serotine bats among others. Wild boar are found all over Poland, and the European bison – Europe's largest mammal – live there in reserves. Other larger mammals in Poland include the European lynx, beaver, grey wolf, and elk.

Many unusual birds live in Poland, including the white-tailed eagle and the corncrake. More white storks nest in Poland than anywhere else in the world. Other bird species include the white-backed woodpecker, hazel grouse, aquatic warbler, red-breasted flycatcher, cranes, and golden eagles.

How to say...

bat *nietoperz* (nye-TOP-ezh)
beaver *bóbr* (BOO-br)
bison *bizon* (BEE-zon)
eagle *orzeł* (O-zhew)

lynx *ryś* (rish)
stork *bocian* (BO-chyan)
wild boar *dzik* (dzheek)
wolf *wilk* (veelk)

Threatened species

A number of **endangered** birds live in Poland, such as the corncrake, Dalmatian pelican, and Egyptian vulture. Various rare moths, butterflies, and beetles are also threatened species. Endangered mammals include the Alpine shrew, the Eurasian bison, the European mink, and some types of bat.

Most of these creatures have become threatened because their **habitats** have been destroyed or developed by humans. Conservation areas are being set up to protect these birds and animals and increase their numbers.

The environment

During Poland's decades of **communist** rule great damage was done to the water, air, and soil in Poland. Many trees were destroyed by acid rain. It is hard to reverse this problem because the industry that powers the country's **economy** is the main cause of pollution.

In 1991, five official **ecological** disaster areas were identified in Poland. The industrial region of Silesia was the most polluted. During the early 1990s, many environmental pressure groups were set up to tackle these environmental problems. Today, politicians and most people in Poland are aware of the issues and the need to protect the environment.

MAŁGORZATA GÓRSKA

The conservationist Małgorzata Górska won the 2010 Goldman Environmental prize for her work protecting Poland's environment. She led protests against a planned road development through the Rospuda Valley in north-east Poland. This land is one of the last real **wilderness** areas left in Europe. Górska's successful fight has protected forests and wetlands, and the species that live there.

The Dalmatian pelican is the rarest species of pelican in the world.

Infrastructure: head of state, homes, and hospitals

Poland is a **republic** that is run as a parliamentary democracy. This type of government allows its people to vote for a president and representatives from a range of political parties. The president is the country's **head of state**, and holds the post for five years. The head of government is the prime minister, who is appointed by the president. He or she runs the government with a council of ministers.

The Polish parliament is made up of a 460-member lower house *(Sejm)* and a 100-member senate *(Senat)*. The country is divided into 16 provinces called *voivodships*. Each has a governor and an elected regional assembly.

This map shows the 16 provinces (*voivodships*) in Poland.

Money

The **currency** in Poland is the *złoty* (zł), which means "golden". There are 100 *grosze* in each *złoty*. There are currently 1, 2, 5, 10, 20, and 50 *groszy* coins, and 1, 2, and 5 *złoty* coins. Banknotes come in 10, 20, 50, 100, and 200 *złoty* **denominations**. Poland will eventually replace the *złoty* with the **euro**, but the **economy** will need to develop further before this is possible.

The pictures on Polish *złoty* show famous people from the country's history.

PRINCE MIESZKO I (C.AD930–992)

On the 10-*złoty* note there is a picture of Prince Mieszko I. He is thought to be the first ruler of a Polish nation. He fought many wars during his reign and gained new lands for Poland. When he married he converted to Christianity, preventing other powers from attacking Poland. His tomb can be found in Poznań Cathedral.

School

Polish children attend primary school for six years and then go to a school called a gymnasium for three years. Pupils go on to a secondary school called a lyceum for three years, or a technical school for four years. There are also basic **vocational** schools where pupils can train for a specific job.

Pre-school education (*wychowanie przedszkolne*) is part of the system of education in Poland. There is a well-established network of state pre-schools that children may attend between the ages of three and six. School education before seven years old is not compulsory, but currently 97 per cent of the nation's children attend.

Children start primary school at the age of seven and the school year runs from September to June. The school day begins at 8.00 a.m. and there is a snack break during the morning. The school day finishes at 1.00 or 2.00 p.m., and in the afternoon many children take music, English language, or sports lessons. They also have homework to do. There are holidays at Christmas and a two-week winter break in January or February.

These Polish children are working hard at school.

Health

Healthcare, including dental care, in Poland is provided for everyone by the government. Every working person contributes tax towards this. Polish medical facilities are good, although they are often better in cities than in some **rural** areas. Private healthcare is also available and some people choose to pay for this to avoid waiting for treatment. The World Health Organization (WHO) placed Poland 50th out of 190 countries in its ranking of world health systems in 2000.

Polish people don't have to pay when they visit the dentist.

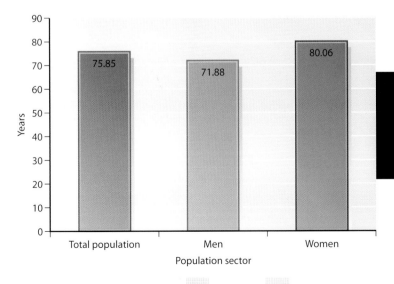

This bar chart shows the life expectancy of people in Poland.

Culture: mazurka, animation, and mushrooms

Music is important in Poland, from traditional folk music to **classical** and modern rock music. Folk dances, such as the mazurka and polonaise, are still popular. Fryderyk Szopen (Frédéric Chopin, 1810–1849) is the most famous Polish classical composer. He was a great pianist and most of his works were written for the piano.

More recently, the composer Zbigniew Preisner has written award-winning music for films by Polish directors such as Krzysztof Kieślowski and Agnieszka Holland.

Literature

In the 1800s, a group of Polish poets wrote **patriotic** poetry. Adam Mickiewicz, Juliusz Slowacki, and Zygmunt Krasiński were called the Three Bards and helped to keep Polish identity alive. Several Poles have won the **Nobel Prize** for Literature, such as Henryk Sienkiewicz (1905), Czeslaw Milosz (1980), and Wislawa Szymborska (1996), who is one of few women poets to ever win the prize.

HANNA KRALL (1937–)

The Jewish writer Hanna Krall often writes about the terrible suffering of Jewish Poles during World War II. She herself was hidden from the **Nazis** and saved from being sent to a **concentration camp**. However, many of her relatives were killed.

This painting, *The Constitution of the 3rd May 1791* by Jan Matejko shows an important event in Polish and Lithuanian history.

Art

During the 1800s, artists such as Jan Matejko (1838–1893) painted typical Polish traditions and events from the nation's history. Another artist, Józef Marian Chełmoński (1849–1914) painted scenes of Polish nature.

YOUNG PEOPLE

There are several big music festivals in Poland that attract young people from across Europe. The Opole Festival particularly celebrates Polish pop music, while the Open'er and Sopot Festivals attract more international artists. Globaltica is a popular festival of world music.

Theatre and film

In the 1800s, there was a strong tradition of Jewish theatre, but wars and **communism** virtually destroyed this. Today, the Kaminska State Jewish Theatre is still performing in Warsaw.

Polish directors and actors often work both on stage and in films. Some famous Polish directors include Andrzej Maleszka, who created many imaginative films for young people, and Agnieszka Holland, who directed *The Secret Garden*.

A Polish filmmaker named Wladyslaw Starewicz, created **stop motion animation** in the early 1900s. He used dolls and insects as the characters in his films. The stop-motion technique is still used in many modern films, such as *Coraline*, which was made in 2009.

Sport

Popular activities in Poland include football, cycling, hiking, and skiing. Some famous Polish sportspeople include Tomasz Gollob who races in motorcycle speedway, the tennis player Agnieszka Roma Radwańska, and Tomasz Kuszczak who has played as goalkeeper for Manchester United.

Agnieszka Radwańska plays tennis at the highest level.

Leisure

People in Polish towns and cities enjoy going to concerts, the cinema, and theatres. Around 58.4 per cent of the population is connected to the internet and young people enjoy playing computer games. Most Polish people spend a lot of time with their families. In the countryside, people enjoy watersports, skiing, and hiking. Picking mushrooms is also a popular activity in the countryside during the autumn.

These skiers are enjoying the slopes in the Tatra Mountains.

Daily life

It is normal for Poles to use more **formal** language when they speak to older people and people in authority. It is also a custom for people to take off their shoes when they go into someone's home. Often hosts provide slippers for guests to wear.

Traditions

The Feast of Greenery is a bit like a harvest festival and takes place on 8 September. Farmers take bouquets of herbs and vegetables to churches to be blessed and then keep them on display at home. On 1 and 2 November many Polish people visit cemeteries to light candles and remember dead friends and relatives.

Wigilia is a vegetarian feast held on Christmas Eve. Families eat together after the first star has been spotted in the sky. It is traditional to have an even number of guests and an extra place is laid in case a guest arrives. On Christmas Day, children in **rural** areas often walk around singing carols and carrying nativity scenes.

Food

Traditional Polish meals tend to be very meat-based and filling. Popular dishes include soups, stew, sausages, and *pierogi* – small dumplings like ravioli, stuffed with meat, mushrooms, cheese, or fruit (see the recipe on page 33 to try it out for yourself). *Gołąbki* are rolled-up cabbage leaves filled with meat and rice. Polish people enjoy cakes and pastries for dessert.

How to say...

apple *jabłko* (YAH-pw-koh)
beetroot *burak* (BOO-rahk)
bread *chleb* (hleb) bread
cabbage *kapusta* (kah-POO-stah)
cake *ciastko* (CHYAST-ko)
meat *mięso* (MYE(ng)-so)
milk *mleko* (MLE-ko)
potato *ziemniak* (ZYEHM-nyahk)
sausage *kiełbasa* (kye(w)-BA-sa)
soup *zupa* (ZOO-pa)

Potato pierogi

Ask an adult to help you make this delicious snack.

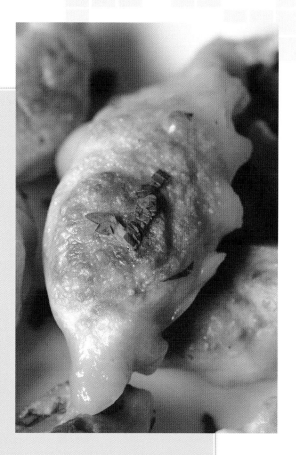

Ingredients:

Dough
- 3 eggs
- 225 ml soured cream
- 375 g plain flour
- ¼ teaspoon salt
- 1 tablespoon baking powder

Filling
- 80 g butter
- 150 g chopped onion
- 800 g cold mashed potato

What to do:

1. First prepare the filling. Melt the butter in a frying pan and add the onion. Cook for about 5 minutes, then add to the mashed potato.
2. Next, make the dough. Beat the eggs and sour cream together. Mix the flour, salt, and baking powder together and stir into the cream mixture.
4. Knead the dough and roll it out flat on to a floured surface. Cut out circles of dough.
5. Put a small spoonful of filling into the middle of the circles. Brush water on to the edges of the circles and fold them over. Press the edges together.
6. Add the pierogi to a pan of boiling water and cook for around 5 minutes.
7. Remove and serve.

Poland today

Since the end of **communism** Poland has generally enjoyed success. The country's **economy** has improved, with new businesses starting up and new, modern buildings changing city skylines. Membership of the **EU** means that young Polish people can travel and work in many other countries. Tourism is flourishing, particularly in the historic cities and beautiful coastal regions.

However, more still needs to be done to modernize all areas of the country. The global economic crisis that started in 2008 has hit Poland along with the rest of Europe. They were also hit by tragedy in 2010 when a plane carrying the Polish president, Lech Kaczynski, and other government officials crashed, killing all 96 people on board.

Despite these setbacks, Poland can look forward to a positive future. Visitors to Poland can enjoy the experience of beautiful beaches, mountains, forests, and wilderness, as well as bustling cities and traditional villages. Polish people are well known for their warmth and hospitality. Why not find out more about this fascinating and varied country and its friendly people?

How to say...

Hi! *cześć!* (tsheshts)
Hello *dzień dobry* (dzeyhn DOH-bri)
How are you? *jak się masz?* (yahk shyeh mahsh)
Goodbye *do widzenia* (do vee-DZEN-ya)
Thank you *dziekuje* (dzeng-KOO-yeh)
Please/you're welcome *proszę* (PROH-sheng)
Yes *tak* (tahk)
No *nie* (nyeh)

The former **pope**, John Paul II, was one of Poland's most famous people. He was born Karol Józef Wojtyła in a village near Kraków. His visits to the country as pope helped to speed up the changes that led to the end of communism.

Fact file

Official name:	**Republic** of Poland
Official language:	Polish
Capital city:	Warsaw
Bordering countries:	Belarus, Czech Republic, Germany, Lithuania, Russia, Slovakia, Ukraine
Population:	38,463,689
Largest cities (population):	Warsaw (1,711,466)
	Kraków (754,854)
	Łódź (744,541)
	Wrocław (632,240)
Urban population:	61 per cent of total population
Birth rate:	10.04 births per 1,000 people
Life expectancy (total):	75.63 years
Life expectancy (men):	71.65 years
Life expectancy (women):	79.85 years
Religion (percentage):	Roman Catholic (89.8%)
	Eastern Orthodox (1.3%)
	Protestant (0.3%)
	other or unspecified (8.6%)
Internet users:	22,450,600 (58.4% of total population)
Military service:	9 months for males aged 18–28
Type of government:	multi-party parliamentary **democracy**
National animal:	white eagle
National tree:	alder
Climate:	cold winters and mild to hot summers, with frequent rain in summer and winter
Area (total):	312,685 square kilometres (120,728 square miles)
Land:	304,255 square kilometres (117,473 square miles)
Water:	8,430 square kilometres (3,254 square miles)

Mountains:	Rysy – 2,499 metres (8,199 feet)
	Turbacz – 1,315 metres (4,314 feet)
Major rivers:	Wisła – 1,047 kilometres (650.5 miles)
	Warta – 808 kilometres (502 miles)
	Oder (within Poland) – 742 kilometres (461 miles)
Highest point:	Rysy – 2,499 metres (8,199 feet)
Lowest point:	near Raczki Elblaskie – -2 metres (-6.5 feet)
Currency:	*złoty*
Natural resources:	coal, sulphur, copper, natural gas, silver, lead, salt, **amber**, arable land
Major industries:	machine building, iron and steel, coal mining, chemicals, shipbuilding, food processing, glass, beverages, textiles
Main imports:	machinery, manufactured goods, chemicals, minerals, fuels, lubricants
Main exports:	machinery, manufactured goods, food, live animals
Units of measurement:	metric

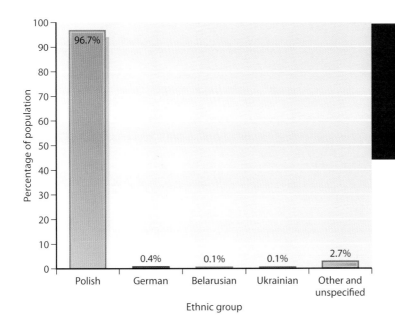

This bar graph shows that most people in Poland are of the Polish ethnic group.

Famous Poles

Nicolaus Copernicus (astronomer),
Marie Curie (chemist and physicist),
Fryderyk Szopen (musician and composer),
Jan Pieńkowski (children's book author and illustrator),
Agnieszka Holland (film director),
Krzysztof Kieślowski (film director),
Max Factor (born as Max Faktor, cosmetics businessman),
Lech Wałęsa (politician),
Karol Józef Wojtyła (**Pope** John Paul II),
Barbara Trzetrzelewska (pop singer),
Agnieszka Radwańska (tennis player)

Poland's national anthem

These are the first two verses and the chorus of the Polish national anthem
Mazurek Dąbrowskiego (Dąbrowski's Mazurka):

> *Poland has not yet perished.*
> *As long as we live,*
> *What foreign violence has seized,*
> *With sabres in hand we will retrieve.*
>
> *Cross the Vistula and Warta*
> *We shall be Poles;*
> *Bonaparte has shown us*
> *The way to victory.*

Chorus:
> *March! March, Dabrowski!*
> *From Italy to Poland!*
> *Under your command*
> *Unite us as a people.*

Many Poles enjoy holidays in resorts such as Sopot, on the Pomeranian coast.

National holidays

1 January	New Year's Day
March/April	Easter
1 May	May Day
3 May	Constitution Day
15 August	Feast of the Assumption
1 November	All Saints' Day
11 November	Independence Day
25–26 December	Christmas

Timeline

BC is short for "before Christ". BC is added after a date and means that the date occurred before the birth of Jesus Christ, for example, 450 BC.

AD is short for *Anno Domini*, which is Latin for "in the year of our Lord". AD is added before a date and means that the date occurred after the birth of Jesus Christ, for example, AD 720.

966	Mieszko I becomes the first ruler of a united Poland
1241	The Mongols invade Poland. The city of Kraków is destroyed.
1320	Wladislaw the Elbow-High becomes king. Kraków becomes the capital city of Poland.
1333	Kazimierz the Great becomes king
1386	Queen Jadwiga marries Lithuanian Duke Jagiełło, uniting the two countries
1493	First parliament held in Poland
1543	Nicolaus Copernicus publishes his ideas about Earth revolving around the Sun
1655	Sweden invades Poland, marking the start of the five-year Deluge
1700	Start of 21-year war against Sweden
1772	Austria, **Prussia**, and Russia make an agreement to divide Poland between them. The division is complete by 1795.
1815	Poland becomes a kingdom
1898	Marie Curie and Pierre Curie discover the new element polonium

1914	World War I begins
1918	World War I ends
1939	**Nazi** Germany invades Poland. World War II begins.
1942	Nazis begin to use **concentration camps** in Poland to kill European **Jews**
1943	Warsaw **Ghetto** uprising takes place when Jewish fighters resist the Nazis for four weeks
1944	Warsaw Uprising takes place when Polish resistance fighters battle the Nazis in Warsaw for two months
1945	World War II ends with much of Poland destroyed
1947	A **communist** government is elected in Poland
1956	Poznań strikes take place, protesting against low wages
1979	**Pope** John Paul II visits Poland
1980	Workers are allowed to form a **trade union** called Solidarity. It is banned in 1981.
1989	Solidarity is made legal again. Solidarity wins the election.
1990	Solidarity leader Lech Wałęsa is elected President
1999	Poland joins **NATO**
2003	Polish troops join the invasion of Iraq
2004	Poland joins the **EU**
2007	The Polish government collapses and elections are held
2010	President of Poland, Lech Kaczynski, is killed in a plane crash

Glossary

ally country that has agreed to help another country, usually to fight wars against a shared enemy

amber orangey-red stone used in jewellery

astronomy study of planets and stars

biosphere reserve protected natural area

bureaucracy organization with too much power or too many rules

Christian related to the religion based on the teachings of Christ, or a person of that religion

classical serious, artistic music, often played by an orchestra or piano

communism social system where all people in a country share work and property. People who practise communism are called communists.

concentration camp prison and death camps where people were sent during World War II

controversial likely to result in different opinions

culture practices, traditions, and beliefs of a society

currency banknotes and coins accepted in exchange for goods and services

democratic type of government that is elected by a country's people

denomination unit of value in a currency

ecological related to how plants and animals interact

economy to do with the money, industry, and jobs in a country

endangered in danger of extinction

euro type of currency used in many European countries

EU (European Union) organization of European countries with shared political and economic aims

export transport and sell goods to another country

famine serious widespread shortage of food

formal following polite forms and behaviours

ghetto area in a city where a minority group lives separately

habitat environment where a plant or animal lives

head of state main public representative of a country, such as a queen or president

infrastructure networks and structures needed for a society to function, such as roads, power supplies, communications, and buildings

Jew person of the Jewish religion, ethnicity, or culture. Jewish people trace their roots back to the ancient Hebrew people of Israel.

migrate move from one part of the world to another in order to settle there

NATO (North Atlantic Treaty Organization) organization that includes the United States, Canada, and many European countries in which members give each other military help

Nazi member of the National Socialist Party in Germany in the 1930s and 1940s

Nobel Prize award given every year to people who have made outstanding achievements in the fields of peace, literature, science, and economics

patriotic full of love for one's home country

plain area of low, flat land

pope leader of the Roman Catholic church

Prussia kingdom that was part of the German Empire from 1701 to 1918

radioactive substance that gives off energy produced by its atoms

republic country with an elected leader and no monarch

recession decline in business and industry

rural in the countryside

Soviet Union communist state made up of Russia and its former empire, in existence between 1922 and 1991

stop motion animation where puppets are moved bit by bit and filmed to capture each stage of the action

trade union organized group of workers

tribe independent social group, historically often made up of nomadic peoples

UNESCO (United Nations Educational, Scientific, and Cultural Organization) agency that helps countries to work together through education, science, and culture

urban relating to cities and large towns

vocational related to a profession or occupation

Find out more

Books

Children's History of the 20th Century (Dorling Kindersley, 1999)

Cooking the Polish Way, Danuta Zamojska Hutchins (Lerner Publishing Group, 2009)

National Geographic Kids World Atlas (National Geographic Society, 2010)

The Silver Sword, Ian Serraillier (Red Fox, 2003)

The Usborne Encyclopedia of World History, Jane Bingham, Fiona Chandler, and Sam Taplin (Usborne, 2009)

Websites

www.polishculture.org.uk

This website for the Polish Cultural Institute in London has lots of information about Polish culture, and will also help you find out more about Polish people in the United Kingdom.

poland.embassyhomepage.com

Visit the website of the Polish Embassy in London to see maps of Poland and find out about Polish weather, holidays, money, and language.

www.poland.travel/en-gb

Poland's official travel website has plenty of information about places to visit.

https://www.cia.gov/library/publications/the-world-factbook/geos/pl.html

Visit the online CIA World Fact Book to find out everything you need to know about Poland.

education.stateuniversity.com/pages/1212/Poland-PREPRIMARY-PRIMARY-EDUCATION.html#ixzz0yyIPgQvX

Visit this website to find out more about the Polish education system.

Places to visit

If you ever get the chance to go to Poland, here are just some of the many places you could visit:

Warsaw parks

Visit Agrykola Park in Warsaw to relax on the grass, kick a ball around, or enjoy concerts and other events. Lazienki Park has a lake where you can take a boat trip and see a former royal palace. Powsin Park has cycle paths, tennis courts, and botanical gardens.

Mazury Lakes

This is an area of lakes in Warminsko-Mazurskie province. You can go sailing or canoeing here, or enjoy bird watching and picnics.

Beaches

The beaches on the Baltic coast of Pomerania are large white sandy beaches next to pine forests. Explore the sand dunes in Słowiński National Park or have a seaside holiday in the village of Mielno.

Malbork Castle

Explore this huge fortress in the town of Malbork on the banks of the River Wisła. You can check out the drawbridge and moat as well as the many winding corridors and chambers inside.

Canal trips

There are plenty of opportunities for barge and boating holidays all over Poland, particularly in the north-east where there are many canal systems. If you want a really unique experience, try a trip on the Elblag Canal. At one point in the 11-hour journey, the canal boat travels over fields on rails!

Topic tools

You can use these topic tools for your school projects. Trace the map on to a sheet of paper, using the thick black outlines to guide you.

The red colour in the Polish flag represents strength and bravery, while the white stands for peace and honesty. Copy the flag design and then colour in your picture. Make sure you use the right colours!

N

■ Warsaw

Index